How to Ruin YOUR Children's LIVES

D0831414

How to Ruin YOUR Children's LIVES

Mary McHugh

Illustrations by Adrienne Hartman

Andrews McMeel Publishing

Kansas City

Dedicated with love to Alexandra and Leigh Haley
—*Adrienne Hartman*

. . . and to my daughter, Karen, who refused to be ruined
—*Mary McHugh*

04 05 06 07 08 TNS 10 9 8 7 6 5 4 3 2 1

ISBN: 0-7407-4708-8

Library of Congress Control Number: 2004102695

Attention: Schools and Businesses:
Andrews McMeel books are available at quantity discounts with bulk purchase for educational, business, or sales promotional use. For information, please write to: Special Sales Department, Andrews McMeel Publishing, 4520 Main Street, Kansas City, Missouri 64111.

Sometimes it seems as if teenagers are from another planet. They used to be such reasonable children, such delightful little people who thought we were wonderful. They were loving and worshipful and brought joy into our hearts each day as we sent them off into the world, confident in our brilliance as parents.

Then—Something Happened. They suddenly turned into hostile creatures who wanted as little to do with us as possible. It happened around the age of eleven or twelve and continued until they went off to college or out to work, and we suppressed feelings of relief that they were gone.

Sooner or later, every parent is bound to hear the words (usually screamed from another room) "You're ruining my life!" Perhaps you are. But if you feel your child-ruining skills are slipping, here are some helpful tips:

Repeat often with a sigh,
"Youth is wasted on the young."

When your teenager listens to
"Just Let Me Cry" for the hundredth time,
make an appointment for her
with a psychiatrist.

When your daughter says,
"You love my brother more than me!" say,
"I was hoping you wouldn't find out."

Scream and slam the door when your daughter's date for the evening shows up in an undershirt with tattoos covering every inch of his body.

If your teenager stops talking to you, give a special prayer of thanks to God.

Say you had a better career in mind than
a garage mechanic when your teenager says
he doesn't want to go to college.

Fool yourself into thinking
that you can protect your teenager from
every disappointment in life.

Return all your daughter's thongs and replace
them with large white underpants.

Pretend that seventh grade will be
one of the best years of your teenager's life.

Get your picture on the front page
of the local paper being arrested
during a peace march.

Say, "Why can't you be like Sam?
He tells his mother *everything*."

Wish your teenagers were like
your best friend's teens. (The truth is,
they're not so great either.)

Refuse to let them go to a party at any house where there is a convicted felon in residence.

Ask for the "bored teenager" menu when you go out to eat.

Expect them to get up the first time you call them in the morning.

Disregard the sign on your teenager's door:
DANGER. KEEP OUT. THAT MEANS YOU.
OFF LIMITS.

Meditate when chaos is all around you.
They hate that.

Put in ear plugs when they learn to say,
"You're ruining my life!"

Forget what it was like to go to school
and see a girl you hate
wearing the same shirt you have on.

Say to a starving teenaged boy,
"Don't eat that cookie. You'll spoil your
appetite for dinner."

When your daughter comes home suicidal
because some boy rejected her, say,
"There are lots of fish in the sea."

Come unglued when you find a Victoria's Secret
catalog under your son's bed.

Read your daughter's diary and ask her about the juicy parts.

Kiss your date good night in front of your kids after your divorce. Better still, marry him.

Take their bedroom door off its hinges if your
teenagers have locked it to keep you out.

Say, "If you say 'totally' one more time
I'm going to a sanatorium."

Don't assume that just because your daughter's
eye makeup makes her look like Dracula doesn't
mean she will bite someone's neck.

Understand that your daughter's
"I promise to do better" really means
"I need a ride to the mall."

Think they will be fascinated by anything you
did that day, including organizing a fair
that raised $10,000 for the school library.

Expect them to be interested in whatever your husband or you have to say at dinner.

Think they have the same sense of time that you have, i.e., that they'll get somewhere when they are supposed to.

Do not appreciate the fact that her hair is the most important topic of conversation almost any day of the year.

Blame peer pressure for rudeness, strange piercings, smoking, tattoos, total noncommunication, hostile stares, and bad breath.

Refuse to be a slave.

Have a life of your own.

Think "Whatever!" is a friendly remark.

Love them no matter what they do.

Consider rejection a rite of passage and stay calm.
They hate that.

Smile when your teenager says,
"If anything goes wrong, it's your fault."

Say, "Why can't you be like Jennifer?
Her room is always neat as a pin."

Say, "You're *not* getting a cell phone
that takes pictures."

Expect them to notice and say
something nice when you've spent three hours
making a boeuf bourguignon.

Tell them a growing boy needs at least
eight hours sleep.

Laugh when your daughter tells you
what she has learned in psychology class
about parenting. Say, "Good luck!"

Bring up your teenager's D in history
at the dinner table.

Make meal time a synonym for "lecture time."

Say, "We used to have such fun when you were a little girl and had tea parties together."

Faint when your son tells you he has joined the Young Republicans club.

Fall asleep when your teenager is telling you what
Sue said to Jennifer and what Jennifer told
Maryanne and what Karen did then.

Run out on the basketball court
with a first-aid kit if your teenager is hurt
during a game.

Expect them to introduce their friends to you.

Underestimate the importance of being
in the right clique.

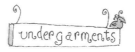

Fail to understand the importance
of big breasts.

Consider motorcycles an invention
of the devil.

When all else fails, just say loudly,
"Because I said so."

Say, "Don't use that tone with me,"
and expect it to have some effect.

Think you understand what is
going on in their minds.

Expect them to say "Thank you" and "Please"
once they've reached thirteen.

Miss the point that they can eat at
McDonald's, Burger King, and Pizza Hut
every day and not gain an ounce.

Say, "It isn't always about you!"

Call them at their friend's house to ask
if they want lasagna for dinner.

Tell them they must be at least thirty
before they can get their belly button pierced.

Say, "I'm doing this for your own good."

Ask them about girlfriends (or boyfriends)
in front of relatives.

Say, "You will thank me later for this."

Attempt to draw their friends
into a conversation.

Get really fat.

Drop them off where their friends can see you.

Talk about anything at all when you are driving your child and his friends somewhere.

Expect them to take coherent phone messages.

Pretend you like what passes
for music in their world.

Explain to them that because the prefrontal
cortex in their brain has not yet developed,
they do not know how to control their
emotions, restrain harmful impulses, or
make rational decisions.

Ask them "Why?" as in "Why did you eat
a peanut butter and jelly sandwich on my
new couch?" or "Why did you back our car
into that stone wall?"

Expect an answer to
"Have you done your homework?"

Say, "Hi dude, nice threads,"
to your son's friend when he comes
to your house in a clean T-shirt.

Say "dude" for any reason whatsoever.

Tell them about the evils of pot
while you're sipping a Cosmo.

Say, "I'll treat you like an adult
when you *act* like an adult."

Say, "How can you listen to Eminem—
he's so mean to his mother."

Tell your daughter one hole in each earlobe is enough for anybody.

Assume that they will be the way they are at fifteen for the rest of their lives.

Take them down to the basement and explain
what the washer and dryer are for.

Move to Vermont and don't leave a
forwarding address.

Say, "Breakfast is the most important meal
of the day" as they're gulping down half
a glass of orange juice on their
way out the door.

Suggest that some other color than black
might be a better choice for the walls
of their rooms.

Start a discussion of possible college choices
on the way to a basketball game.

Say, "I told you when we got that dog
that he was your responsibility."

Insist that they get home before 3 a.m.

Say, "Whatever happened to my happy, smiling, little boy (or girl)?"

Remain calm and reasonable while they
are telling you what a terrible parent you are.

Refer to Fifty Cent as Fifty Cents
and ask who shot him nine times.

Repeat everything at least five times
so they'll really get the message.

Bring up Monica Lewinsky whenever
you are having a frank talk about sex
with your teenager.

Ruffle your teenager's hair while you're waiting to buy tickets in the movie line.

Spit on a Kleenex and rub the chocolate off your teenager's chin in public.

Hint that you and your spouse
are still having sex.

Serve a very rare steak for dinner the day
she decides to become a vegetarian.

Wear your mink coat the day she joins PETA.

Insist that her jeans cover her cleavage in back.

Scream that you don't care if her best friend's
mother is letting her get breast implants
at fourteen, she is not getting them.

Tell your son that you are afraid someone will get hurt on the spikes in his hair.

Explain in a very loud voice that your
daughter cannot go to school
in clothes that look like underwear.

Point out that perhaps Kelly and Jack Osborne
are not the best role models to follow.

Complain that your teenager hasn't
left his room for three days and
that it smells funny in there.

Suggest that your daughter's new friend
who always carries condoms in her purse
might not be the best person to hang out with.

Say, "When you have children of your own,
you'll understand why I'm doing this."

Ask, "What's a Justin Timberlake?"

Call them teddy bear or honey bee in public.

Put the birthday money from
their grandparents in the college fund
instead of letting them spend it on CDs.

Put a scarf, ear muffs, and tissues
in their pockets on a cold winter morning.

Tell everyone at a dinner party how your son
loved to have his toenails painted red
when he was five.

Tell him not to brag about his grades to
his friends, then brag about his grades
to your friends.

Leave the pimple medication on the kitchen counter when your teen brings home a member of the opposite sex to do homework.

Make them wear more than a T-shirt
when the temperature is below freezing.

Confiscate their fake IDs.

After finding her birth control pills, insist
that your daughter go to a doctor for a checkup.

Cry when they remember your birthday.

Talk to him about sex (because his father won't).

Tell your teenagers how you lost your virginity.
(It could take weeks before they
speak to you again.)

Before their first girl-boy party,
give them your birth control speech.

Tell them they absolutely cannot tell
their younger brother that he was adopted
(when he wasn't).

Tell them they cannot tell their little sister
she is a trade-in for the sister before her
who was bad.

Tell them nobody really needs a cell phone
when there are pay phones available.

Think you're being cool
when you really haven't a clue.

Tell your friends in front of your daughter,
"Jenny and I are more like sisters than
mother and daughter."

Be oblivious to the fact that your days of wearing a belly shirt and low-slung jeans are *way* past.

Ignore the fact that a thirteen-year-old is a whole other child than the one you've always known.

Expect them to go out on group dates
until they are eighteen.

Say, "Those popular kids are all snobs anyway."

Talk about Hogwarts, Quidditch,
and Muggles in front of their friends.

Pretend you *like* watching *Lizzie McGuire*.

Insist, against all odds, that you have a perfect relationship with your teenagers.

Be one of the girls when your daughter has a slumber party.

Expect them to find *your* life interesting when you're on *Oprah,* are awarded the Nobel Prize, or win a tennis championship at Wimbledon.

Wear fishnet stockings to your conference
with their teacher.

Ask them to tell you
what they did in school that day.

Pretend you are not as obsolete
as last year's computer.

Wear an ankle bracelet.

Think of yourself as their best friend,
not their mother.

Shoot collagen into your lips until
they look like Angelina Jolie's.

Quote Howard Stern.

Wear your fur coat to a basketball game.

Expect them to notice you're in the room.

Say in front of your daughter,
"Everyone says we look exactly alike."

Say in front of your son, "Everyone says he
has a personality just like mine."

Say "You're thirty-five years old.
It's time to get an apartment of your own."

Make your child take piano lessons long after
he has proven to have no musical talent at all.

Expect your baseball star daughter
to love ballet the way you did.

Say, "I could have been on Broadway
if I hadn't married and had children."

Show them your favorite moves
when you were a cheerleader in high school—
preferably when they have friends over.

Never say, "I'm sorry. I was wrong."

Expect them to go to the same college you did
even if they hate Ohio.

Tell them their father is an idiot.

Faint when you see men's feet in the shower
in their college dorm.

When you visit them in their own apartment
in the city, tell them that they should
eat more veggies.

Assume your daughter is having sex with
every boy with a tattoo and an earring.

Call them at two in the morning when
they have moved out of the house
to see if they are home yet.

Expect your grown children
to return your phone calls.

Object when they program a different ring
for your cell phone calls so they'll know
it's you and don't answer.

Assume your children *want*
you to call them at work.

Drop in on your adult children
without calling first.

Take them seriously when they tell you
they will *never* treat their own children
the way you treat them.

Be absolutely sure that your daughter will
be pregnant at sixteen the first time she
wears makeup and goes out on a date alone.

Hug your child when she says, "I hate you!"

Think you can fix all their problems
the way you did when they were five.

Believe that saying "No" to your children
will squash their individuality.

Ask your grown daughter if she has to
go to the bathroom when you leave the house.

Talk about dieting all the time.

Say, "If you ever get fat,
I'll come back to haunt you."

Say, "Winning is everything."

Visit your grown daughter in her first apartment
and rearrange all her shelves.

Tell your child you were in excruciating pain
in labor for forty-eight hours
before he was born.

Tell your children they will be total failures
if they don't go to college.

If your son likes to cook, loves musicals,
and is very neat, assume that he's gay.

Tell your children to call you by your first name
so you'll feel younger.

Lie about your age.

Put your plastic surgeon on speed dial.

Express an opinion about anything.

Keep thinking you can win an argument
with your teenagers.

Suggest that nobody looks good in orange
when your daughter is picking out
her bridesmaids' dresses.

Dance by yourself at any function where
your children can see you.

Tell your best friend something your
teenager told you in private.

Tell your daughter every girl
should know how to sew.

Teach your teenager to drive.

Go shopping for anything
with your teenager.

Say, "You have to cover your stomach
when you go to your grandmother's house
for Thanksgiving."

Cut your own hair after three margaritas.

Blame their father for everything
that goes wrong.

Object when your teenager walks
three feet ahead of you in the mall.

Tell your five-year-old she cannot wear
her bathing suit to kindergarten.

Make your children wear a sweater
when you're cold.

Tell your fourteen-year-old she has to have
at least one outfit that isn't black.

Take everything they say personally
and vow to get even.

Keep the same hairdo you had in high school.

Make little screaming noises when
your teenager is driving the car.

When they're driving, say, "Slow down.
Get in the right lane. Don't tailgate.
Watch that car," etc.

Push back a strand of hair from
your teen's forehead in public.

Giggle uncontrollably asking
the guy in the grocery section of the
supermarket if he has any loose nuts
when you're with your teen.

Tap-dance to the music in the supermarket
as you wheel your cart down the aisle
when you're with your teenager.

In church, sing the hymns louder than
anyone else around you.

Call your teens on their cell phones
just to say, "I love you."

Wear lipstick to their next baseball game.

Tell them off-color jokes
in front of their friends.

Be offended when your teenager announces
that she wants to find her real mother
since she obviously must be adopted.

Cultivate a loud, annoying laugh.

Use the kitchen counter as a barre and perform your best ballet pliés for the cat while your teenager is eating lunch.

Find your old guitar and sing "Kumbaya" and "This Land Is Your Land" for your teens and their friends.

Have a high-powered career that keeps you out of the house most of the time.

Don't have any kind of career and stay home with your children all of the time.

Expect them to be adorable when you have friends over for a dinner party.

Dance really weird someplace where your teenagers can see you.

When your daughter brings home a boy
to study with, ask "Are you guys an item?"

Comment on how good-looking some
movie star is in front of your teenager's friends.

Assume your daughter's gloomy poetry
means she is deeply depressed.

Cook Coquilles St. Jacques when their friends
are invited for dinner.

Assume they're homophobic
if they don't like Ellen DeGeneres.

Sing old Beatles songs when their friends
are in the car.

Consider rice cakes a snack.

Drive slower than the speed limit.

Drive faster than the speed limit.

Drive at the speed limit.

Tell them long, boring stories about people they have never heard of.

Insist that they drag their little brother or sister along when they go to the mall.

Tell them the whole world isn't
watching everything they do.

Demand that they join the rest of the family
for dinner.

Say, "What will the neighbors think?"

Dress like Christina Aguilera.

Dress like an old lady.

Dress in moderate-priced clothes.

Dress in expensive clothes.

Don't wear underwear under your clothes.

Have extreme right-wing political views.

Have extreme left-wing political views.

Have no political views.

Have fun.

Tell them about the time you streaked
when you were in college.

Kiss your teenager in public.

Insist they come to church/synagogue/mosque.

Use their slang correctly or incorrectly—
they'll hate you either way.

Say, "Why does that sweet little Britney Spears dress like that?"

Freak out when you discover a pamphlet on Scientology in your teenager's room.

Ask your son, "How was your day?" when he didn't get picked for junior varsity soccer, got a D on his math exam, and is in the third stage of terminal acne.

Keep saying "Cool" after the expression
has changed to "Tight."

Assume that whatever you want to do
is what they want to do.

Point out a girl who would make a great wife
before your teenager is out of eighth grade.

Make them baby-sit their hyper two-year-old
twin cousins who are not out of diapers yet.

Correct their grammar.

Make bad puns.

Tell them they need to go into therapy
whenever they disagree with you.

Explain the facts of life using euphemisms
like "the birds and the bees."

Explain the facts of life clearly and directly.

Explain the facts of life when they are
either too young to understand or are
old enough to know more than you do.

Say you hate *Friends*.

Smoke.

Read their IMs.

Hang nude paintings in the living room.

Wait up for them.

Don't wait up for them.

Remind your daughter that she loved
the beauty parlor when she was five and
she'll love it again when she's twenty-five.

Say to one of their friends,
"My, how you've grown!"

Tell them they are not allowed to lock
their younger sibling out of the house.

Say that a stick of gum does not count as dinner.

Tell your teenager he cannot drop eggs
from a tenth-floor apartment window
as part of a science experiment.

Say you feel sorry for them because they
will never know what it was like to
live in the 1960s.

Make them go to a museum on a Saturday.

Do card tricks for their friends.

Give them an Easter basket when they are eighteen with little marshmallow bunnies in it.

Lecture them on privacy when they know you go through their book bags regularly.

Reveal a secret you didn't know was a secret, like your daughter hates *The Simpsons*.

Tell them if they think putting a condom
on a banana in human relations class has
taught them safe sex to think again.